T0312300

Cambridge Elements ≡

Elements in Law, Economics and Politics

edited by
Series Editor in Chief
Carmine Guerriero, *University of Bologna*
Series Co-Editors
Alessandro Riboni, *École Polytechnique*
Jillian Grennan, *Duke University, Fuqua School of Business*
Petros Sekeris, *Montpellier Business School*

MORE IS LESS

Why Parties May Deliberately Write Incomplete Contracts

Maija Halonen-Akatwijuka
University of Bristol

Oliver Hart
Harvard University

CAMBRIDGE
UNIVERSITY PRESS

CAMBRIDGE
UNIVERSITY PRESS

Shaftesbury Road, Cambridge CB2 8EA, United Kingdom

One Liberty Plaza, 20th Floor, New York, NY 10006, USA

477 Williamstown Road, Port Melbourne, VIC 3207, Australia

314–321, 3rd Floor, Plot 3, Splendor Forum, Jasola District Centre, New Delhi – 110025, India

103 Penang Road, #05–06/07, Visioncrest Commercial, Singapore 238467

Cambridge University Press is part of Cambridge University Press & Assessment, a department of the University of Cambridge.

We share the University's mission to contribute to society through the pursuit of education, learning and research at the highest international levels of excellence.

www.cambridge.org
Information on this title: www.cambridge.org/9781009475952

DOI: 10.1017/9781009396059

First published 2024

A catalogue record for this publication is available from the British Library.

ISBN 978-1-009-47595-2 Hardback
ISBN 978-1-009-39607-3 Paperback
ISSN 2732-4931 (online)
ISSN 2732-4923 (print)

Cambridge University Press & Assessment has no responsibility for the persistence or accuracy of URLs for external or third-party internet websites referred to in this publication and does not guarantee that any content on such websites is, or will remain, accurate or appropriate.

More Is Less

Why Parties May Deliberately Write Incomplete Contracts

Elements in Law, Economics and Politics

DOI: 10.1017/9781009396059
First published online: April 2024

The co-editors in charge of the Halonen-Hart submissions were
Jillian Grennan and Carmine Guerriero.

Maija Halonen-Akatwijuka
University of Bristol

Oliver Hart
Harvard University

Author for correspondence: Maija Halonen-Akatwijuka,
maija.halonen@bristol.ac.uk

Abstract: Why are contracts incomplete? Transaction costs and bounded rationality cannot be a total explanation since states of the world are often describable, foreseeable, and yet are not mentioned in a contract. Asymmetric information theories also have limitations. We offer an explanation based on "contracts as reference points". Including a contingency of the form, "The buyer will require a good in event E", has a benefit and a cost. The benefit is that if E occurs there is less to argue about; the cost is that the additional reference point provided by the outcome in E can hinder (re)negotiation in states outside E. We show that if parties agree about a reasonable division of surplus, an incomplete contract is strictly superior to a contingent contract. If parties have different views about the division of surplus, an incomplete contract can be superior if including a contingency would lead to divergent reference points.

This Element also has a video abstract: www.cambridge.org/ELEP_Halonen

Keywords: incomplete contracts, contracts as reference points, renegotiation, shared views, ambiguity

ISBNs: 9781009475952 (HB), 9781009396073 (PB), 9781009396059 (OC)
ISSNs: 2732-4931 (online), 2732-4923 (print)

Contents

1 Introduction

It is generally accepted by both economists and lawyers that almost all contracts are incomplete. It is simply too costly for parties to anticipate the many contingencies that may occur and to write down unambiguously how to deal with them. Contractual incompleteness has been shown to throw light on a number of matters of interest to economists, such as the boundaries of the firm, asset ownership, and the allocation of control and authority.

Yet the million dollar question remains: why are contracts as incomplete as they are? The idea that transaction costs or bounded rationality are a total explanation for this is not convincing. In many situations some states of the world or outcomes are verifiable and easy to describe, appear relevant, and yet are not mentioned in a contract. A leading example is a breach penalty. A contract will usually specify the price the buyer should pay the seller if trade occurs as intended, but may not say what happens if there is a breach or under what conditions breach is justified. Of course, sophisticated parties often do include breach penalties in the form of liquidated damages but this is far from universal.

A second example concerns indexation. Since a worker's marginal product varies with conditions in the industry she works in as well as the economy as a whole, we might expect to see wages being indexed on variables correlated with industry profitability such as share prices or industry or aggregate unemployment, as well as to inflation. Such an arrangement might have large benefits, allowing wages to adjust and avoiding inefficient layoffs and quits of workers (see, e.g., Weitzman [1984] and Oyer [2004]). Yet, the practice does not seem a common one overall.[1] In the 2008 financial crisis many debt contracts were not indexed to the aggregate state of the economy; if they had been the parties might have been able to avoid default, which might have had large benefits both for them and for the economy as a whole. Similarly, in 2020, few contracts had clauses describing what should happen in the event of a pandemic.

How do we explain the omission of contingencies like these from a contract? One possibility is to argue that putting any contingency into a contract is costly – some of these costs may have to do with describing the relevant state of the world in an unambiguous way – and so if a state is unlikely it may not be worth including it (see, e.g., Shavell [1980], Dye [1985]). This is often the position taken in the law and economics literature (see, e.g., Posner [1986], p.82). However, this view is not entirely convincing. First, states of the world such as breach are often not that unlikely and not that difficult to describe.[2] Second, while the financial crisis or a pandemic may have been unlikely ex ante, now

---

[1] However, see Card (1986) on wage indexation in union contracts in North America.

[2] As argued by Ayres and Gertner (1989), p.128, fn177.

that they have happened the possibility of future crises or pandemics seem only too real. Moreover, finding verifiable ways to describe a crisis or pandemic does not seem to be beyond the capability of contracting parties. Thus, one might expect parties to rush to index contracts on such events. We are not aware of any evidence that this is happening.

A second possibility is to appeal to asymmetric information (see, e.g., Spier [1992]).[3] The idea is that suggesting a contingency for inclusion in a contract may signal some private information and this may have negative repercussions. Such an explanation does not seem very plausible in the case of financial crises – where is the asymmetry of information about the prospects of a global crisis? – but it may apply in other cases. For example, if I suggest a (low) breach penalty you may deduce that breach is likely and this may make you less willing to trade with me. Or if you suggest that my wage should fall if an industry index of costs rises I may think that you are an expert economist who already knows that the index is likely to rise.

Even in these cases asymmetric information does not seem to be a complete answer. Asymmetric information generally implies some distortion in a contract but not that a provision will be completely missing. For example, in the well-known Rothschild-Stiglitz (1976) model, insurance companies offer low-risk types less than full insurance to separate them from high-risk types. But the low-risk types are not shut out of the market altogether – they still obtain some insurance (and the high-risk types receive full insurance). Indeed to explain why a contingency might be omitted from a contract, Spier assumes a fixed cost of writing or enforcing contractual clauses in addition to asymmetric information.[4]

In this Element, we offer an alternative and complementary explanation for why verifiable contingencies are omitted based on the theory of contracts as reference points (see Hart and Moore [2008]).[5] In a nutshell this approach takes the view that a contract circumscribes what parties feel entitled to. Parties do not feel entitled to outcomes outside the contract but may feel entitled to different outcomes within the contract. If a party does not receive what he feels entitled to he is aggrieved and shades on performance, creating deadweight losses.

Hart and Moore (2008) suppose that each party feels entitled to the best outcome permitted by the contract and rule out renegotiation. In this Element

---

[3] For related work, see Aghion and Bolton (1987), Ayres and Gertner (1989,1992), and Aghion and Hermalin (1990).

[4] However, see Hartman-Glaser and Hebert (2020) for a model of missing provisions that does not depend on a writing cost.

[5] There are no doubt other reasons why contingencies are left out of contracts. Parties may find it distasteful to talk about bad outcomes, such as breach or default, or mentioning them may suggest or breed a lack of trust. These explanations tend to involve psychological factors; our Element can be seen as one attempt to model such factors.

we relax both these assumptions. We confine attention to initial contracts that specify a single (possibly contingent) trading outcome ex post (so there is no aggrievement or shading with respect to the initial contract). Renegotiation occurs ex post if the trading outcome is inefficient in the contingency that arises. We assume that as a result of a self-serving bias each party feels entitled to more than half of the surplus from renegotiation, causing aggrievement and shading. In addition, there may be disagreement about the reference point for the evaluation of surplus, increasing aggrievement further. We show that adding a verifiable contingency to the contract may increase disagreement about the appropriate reference point in contingencies not covered by the contract. An incomplete contract would then reduce the deadweight losses from renegotiation.

In our model, a buyer wants a particular good or service most of the time but with some probability may require an "add-on". Some states of the world in which the add-on is required are verifiable, but others are not. The question we ask is whether it is better to specify that the add-on should be supplied in the verifiable states or whether it is better to specify the basic good and rely on renegotiation in the event that a change is needed.

Suppose that a contingency not covered by the contract occurs. One party may choose what would have occurred in one verifiable contingency to be the reference point for renegotiation whereas the other party may choose what would have occurred in another verifiable contingency. Thus having contractual outcomes in several contingencies can complicate renegotiation in contingencies not covered by the contract. This is particularly an issue if the parties have relatively similar views about a reasonable division of surplus. Then renegotiation would proceed smoothly with an incomplete contract, while additional reference points drawn from a more complete contract may hinder renegotiation. We will show that the renegotiation-hindering effect can be dominant – and an incomplete contract can be superior – even when the parties have different views about surplus division. This is the case when the reference points are drawn from very divergent additional contingencies.

The problem arises here because there are multiple reference points and the parties may disagree about which is the right one. In our main model we will assume that each party chooses the reference point most favorable to him or her, but we do not need to go this far. Similar (although weaker) results can be obtained even if each party randomized over the reference points.[6]

---

[6] The idea that a contractual provision for another state can affect entitlements in the current state is related to the notion of external reference points in Section V of the Hart–Moore model. In Hart–Moore, comparable transactions – that can be justified as reasonable to outsiders – can influence entitlements in a particular state but Hart–Moore do not analyze the case where contractual provisions in one state affect entitlements in another.

Our approach seems consistent with lawyers' views about contract interpretation. Schwartz and Scott (2010) argue that judicial interpretation should be made on a limited evidentiary basis, the most important element of which is the contract itself. Although Schwartz and Scott (2010) do not consider the issue of contingent clauses it seems likely that a court that focuses on a contract will find a clause governing one contingency relevant for adjudicating another contingency. If the parties do not want this to happen it may be better to leave the contingency out. This is similar to our idea that contracting parties may want to leave a contingency out to reduce argument among themselves.

It should be noted that the Hart–Moore (2008) model, as it stands, cannot explain why easy-to-contract-on contingencies are left out of contracts. The reason is that in Hart–Moore it is supposed that each party feels entitled to the best outcome in each state. In our setup this would imply that when a contingency not covered by the contract occurs, the seller feels entitled to a price equal to the buyer's valuation, while the buyer feels entitled to a price equal to the seller's cost. As the disagreement is already maximal, an additional provision covering another state cannot make the disagreement worse. Thus, it is important as a first step to generalize the Hart–Moore model: we do this by supposing that while the parties feel entitled to more than half of the renegotiation surplus, $\frac{1}{2}(1 + \beta)$, they do not feel entitled to the full surplus, $\beta \in [0, 1)$.

Our Element is related to a number of contributions in the literature. Bernheim and Whinston (1998) show that it can be optimal not to contract on some verifiable aspects of performance to improve unverifiable performance. For example, a buyer and a seller may contract on price but leave quantity unspecified. This partial incompleteness can give the seller an incentive to provide good (unverifiable) quality given that the buyer's demand is increasing in quality. Bernheim and Whinston (1998) focus on verifiable and unverifiable actions and show how discretionary actions can discipline unverifiable actions. Our model focuses on states rather than actions and shows how an additional contingency can lead to more divergent entitlements and greater shading in unverifiable states.

The literature on the interaction of explicit and relational contracts is also related (see, e.g., Baker et al. [1994] and Schmidt and Schnitzer [1995]). In this literature, an explicit contract determines the default position after reneging and can undermine the relational contract governing the relationship if the default position is too attractive. In our approach additional contingencies may hinder renegotiation in an unverifiable state. Kvaløy and Olsen (2009) allow for the parties to improve verifiability by investing in contract design and show how an inferior explicit breach remedy can strengthen the relational contract by limiting the default position.

Bénabou and Tirole (2003, 2006) and Herold (2010) find that a principal may choose to rely completely on intrinsic motivation if explicit incentives would backfire by signaling some adverse information, for example, about the principal's view of the agent's ability, true motivation for good deeds, or distrust. Che and Hausch (1999), Segal (1999), and Hart and Moore (1999) show that it can be better for parties to rely on ex-post negotiation rather than contracting ex ante when the parties make cooperative investments or when the trading environment is complex. These authors do not investigate how including some contingencies affects the outcomes in other ones.

Bajari and Tadelis (2001) develop a model of contractual incompleteness to understand the choice between fixed price and cost plus contracts. They assume that there is a fixed cost of including a contingency in a contract but like the authors just mentioned do not investigate the interaction between contracting on some contingencies and outcomes in others.

Bounded rationality can also lead to incomplete contracts. In Tirole (2009) agents are aware of their cognitive limitations, in the sense that they know that they may not be aware of the best design for the traded good. The agents can invest in finding out about alternative designs. If agents invest little, contracts are incomplete and there is a high probability that the contract has to be renegotiated. However, contracts may also be too complete if too many resources are spent on search to avoid a vulnerable position in renegotiation. In Bolton and Faure-Grimaud (2010) the agents may postpone thinking about unlikely states until later and instead assign control rights, particularly if the agents have aligned interests.

In Anderlini and Felli (1994) bounded rationality constrains contracts to be based on finitely computable states. If the states are undescribable in that manner, and the contract choice process is computable so that the first best contract cannot be approximated, an incomplete contract is optimal.[7] In contrast, our interest is in whether to include a describable event in the contract.

Within the contracts as reference points literature, Halonen-Akatwijuka and Hart (2020) analyze continuing contracts that are incomplete in the sense that they do not specify price or mandate trade in the next period, but entail an understanding that the parties will engage in fair bargaining. One advantage of such a continuing contract is that it is costless to separate when it is efficient to do so. Separation would require costly renegotiation under a long-term contract, while fixing price can lead to costly renegotiation to avoid inefficient separation when trading conditions have changed. Halonen-Akatwijuka and Hart (2020) do not discuss how adding a contingency can affect outcomes in other

---

[7] See also Al Najjar et al. (2006).

contingencies. In Frydlinger et al. (2019) and Frydlinger and Hart (2024) the focus is on using a formal relational contract to create shared views, which will then minimize aggrievement in any renegotiations. In this Element, we take the parties' views as given.

Finally, our approach is quite closely related to Herweg and Schmidt (2015). Their work also depends on the idea that a contract can provide a reference point that may hinder renegotiation. However, they rely on loss aversion rather than aggrievement. A long-term contract is costly when the parties negotiate away from it, incurring losses relative to the reference point. In our model the parties do not renegotiate in a contracted for contingency since the outcome there is efficient, but including the contingency can hinder renegotiation in other states. Herweg and Schmidt (2015) do not focus on the absence of contingencies in a contract.

The Element is organized as follows. We present the model in Section 2. Section 3 analyzes when an incomplete contract is superior to a more complete contract. The model is extended in Section 4. Section 5 contains a discussion of the results and some conclusions.

2 The Model

Throughout the Element we consider a buyer B and a seller S who meet at date 0 and can trade at date 1. We assume a perfectly competitive market at date 0 but that, possibly because of (unmodelled) relationship-specific investments, B and S face bilateral monopoly at date 1. That is, a "fundamental transformation" in the sense of Williamson (1985) occurs. There is symmetric information throughout. B and S are risk neutral and do not face wealth constraints, and there is no discounting.

We suppose that B and S always want to trade a basic widget, but in some states they want an additional component – an "add-on". Both the basic widget and the augmented widget (the basic widget plus the add-on) are *ex-ante* contractible and specific performance is possible (in contrast to Hart and Moore [2008]). What this means is that B and S can at date 0 write contracts of the form, "We will trade the basic widget" or "We will trade the augmented widget", and these will be enforced at date 1: either party can be assessed a sufficiently large penalty for failing to comply.

We shall suppose that it is always efficient for the parties to trade the basic widget, but that it is only sometimes efficient to have the add-on. There are $n + 1$ states. In state s_0, only the basic widget is needed: The cost exceeds the benefit of the add-on. In states $s_1, \ldots, s_n$ the add-on is efficient. We shall suppose that none of the individual states is verifiable, but there is a verifiable event E

that comprises states $s_1, \ldots, s_r$, where $r \in (1, n)$. As we will see below it is important that there is some ambiguity about the verifiable contingency.

The value of the add-on and its cost in state s_i are given by (v_i, c_i). State s_i occurs with probability π_i, where $\pi_i > 0$ for all i.

Let the gains from trading the add-on be denoted by $G_i \equiv v_i - c_i$. As mentioned, we assume

$$G_0 < 0, G_i > 0, i = 1, \ldots, n. \tag{1}$$

We also suppose that the states $s_1, \ldots, s_n$ can be ranked: s_i has a lower value and a lower cost than s_{i+1}:

$$v_i < v_{i+1}, c_i < c_{i+1} \text{ for } i = 1, \ldots, n-1. \tag{2}$$

The role of (2) will become clear later. Furthermore, we say that the extreme states of E, s_1 and s_r, are (strictly) *overlapping* if $v_1 > c_r$, while the states are (weakly) *disconnected* if $v_1 \leq c_r$.

Finally, we assume that E consists of states where the gains from the add-on are relatively low. Specifically, we assume that the maximal G_i in E is strictly smaller than the minimal G_i in $s_{r+1}, \ldots, s_n$:

$$Max_{i=1,\ldots,r} G_i < Min_{i=r+1,\ldots,n} G_i. \tag{3}$$

In Section 4, we analyze the opposite case where E comprises states where the gains from the add-on are relatively high.

There are three leading contracts:

Contract I: "Always trade the basic widget";

Contract C: "Trade the basic widget except in event E where the add-on is included at an extra charge p";

Contract A: "Always trade the augmented widget".[8]

In contrast to Hart and Moore (2008) we allow for renegotiation once the parties learn the state.[9]

---

[8] Another leading contract used in practice is a cost plus contract: The buyer can require the seller to supply the add-on but must pay the seller's incremental cost (possibly marked up); for discussions see Bajari and Tadelis (2001) and Chakravarty and MacLeod (2009). In this Element, we assume that the seller's incremental cost is not verifiable. We also do not consider contracts that grant the buyer the option to buy, or the seller the option to sell, the add-on at a prespecified price. Such contracts may be useful in some situations but they have their own costs. For example, consider a contract that specifies that the add-on will be provided in event E at price p; and sets a price p' at which the add-on can be traded as long as both parties agree if E does not occur, where for some $v_i > p' > c_i$. Such a contract ensures trade of the add-on in s_i where it is efficient but not in s_0 where it is inefficient (one party will refuse to trade since $v_0 < c_0$). The problem with this contract is that, if $v_0 > v_i$ or $c_i > c_0$, the buyer or the seller will be aggrieved when the add-on is not traded in s_0, and will shade with respect to the basic widget (which is traded), creating deadweight losses.

[9] Renegotiation is introduced also in Halonen-Akatwijuka and Hart (2020).

We will suppose that state s_0 is relatively likely, so that contract A will not be optimal. Hence, we will focus on contracts I and C. Our particular interest is whether the more incomplete contract I is superior to the more complete contract C (in the sense that C includes more contingencies).

Let us turn now to the issue of entitlements, aggrievement, and shading.

We suppose that the initial contract is regarded as "fair" since it is negotiated under competitive conditions. However, parties may disagree about what is reasonable within the contract or if it is renegotiated. A party who does not receive what he is entitled to is aggrieved and shades: He performs within the letter rather than the spirit of the contract in a way that hurts the other party. (Shading is noncontractible.) To be more precise, suppose that a party's payoff is y and he feels entitled to x, where $x > y$. Then his aggrievement is $(x-y)$ and he shades to the point where the other party's payoff is reduced by $\theta(x-y)$, where $\theta \in (0, 1)$ is exogenous. Both B and S can shade. Shading does not affect the payoff of the person doing the shading: it simply reduces the payoff of the other party.

In this Element, we will consider only contracts that specify a single trading outcome in each state. Thus, there is no aggrievement with respect to the initial contract. As noted, in contrast to Hart and Moore (2008), we allow for renegotiation. We also generalize Hart and Moore (2008) by supposing that a party does not necessarily feel entitled to the best possible outcome if the contract is renegotiated. In particular, suppose that there are gains from renegotiation equal to G_i. We assume that because of a self-serving bias each party feels entitled to a fraction $\frac{1}{2}(1 + \beta)$ of the gains, where $\beta \in [0, 1)$.[10] To put it another way, they feel that the other party is entitled to a fraction $\frac{1}{2}(1 - \beta)$ of the gains. (Hart and Moore [2008] can be regarded as the limiting case where $\beta = 1$.)

3 Is More Less?

In this section, we compare the incomplete contract I to the more complete contract C.

Contract I: Always trade the basic widget at some agreed-on price

In s_0 the outcome specified by the contract – trade the basic widget – is efficient and so there will be no renegotiation. Since the contract specifies a single outcome, there is nothing to be aggrieved about: each party gets what he feels entitled to, and so there are no deadweight losses from shading.

Consider next state s_i, $i > 0$, where trade of the add-on is efficient. Here, there are gains from renegotiation given by G_i. Due to self-serving bias each party

---

[10] Assuming symmetric bias is without loss of generality.

feels entitled to a fraction $\frac{1}{2}(1+\beta)$ of the gains. Thus, S feels entitled to a price p'_S for the add-on such that

$$p'_S - c_i = \frac{1}{2}(1+\beta)G_i. \tag{4}$$

B has a similar self-serving bias and thinks he should get $\frac{1}{2}(1+\beta)G_i$ or, equivalently, feels entitled to a price p'_B such that S gets $\frac{1}{2}(1-\beta)G_i$,

$$p'_B - c_i = \frac{1}{2}(1-\beta)G_i. \tag{5}$$

In other words, when the parties take "trade the basic widget" mandated by the contract as the reference point, the reference prices for S and B, derived from (4) and (5) are given by

$$p'_S = c_i + \frac{1}{2}(1+\beta)G_i, \tag{6}$$

$$p'_B = c_i + \frac{1}{2}(1-\beta)G_i. \tag{7}$$

Without loss of generality, suppose that the parties have equal bargaining power, and so they compromise on a 50:50 split of G_i. Each party is then aggrieved by $\frac{1}{2}\beta G_i$.[11] Thus, S will shade to the point where B's payoff falls by $\frac{1}{2}\theta\beta G_i$ and B will shade equally. Total deadweight losses from shading in state s_i equal[12]

$$\theta\beta G_i = \theta(p'_S - p'_B). \tag{8}$$

Note that the total aggrievement is equal to the difference in the two parties' reference prices, $p'_S - p'_B$.

Thus, we can write the expected deadweight losses from contract I as

$$L_I = \sum_{i=1}^{n} \pi_i \theta\beta G_i. \tag{9}$$

Contract C: Trade the basic widget except in event E where the add-on is included at an extra charge p

Contract C introduces additional reference points, and as we shall see this may cause problems.

---

[11] The total deadweight losses do not depend on the 50:50 split. For example, if B can make a take-it-or-leave-it offer, he would offer $\frac{1}{2}(1-\beta)G_i$ to S and S would be aggrieved by βG_i.

[12] Note that we assume that renegotiation does not cause parties to reassess the fairness of the initial contract for the basic widget. For some experimental evidence consistent with this, see Fehr et al. (2015).

Under contract C there is no aggrievement in states $s_0, \ldots, s_r$ since the contract mandates a single outcome that is efficient: basic widget in s_0 and add-on in $s_1, \ldots, s_r$. Thus, the only problem states are $s_{r+1}, \ldots, s_n$ where the contract mandates the basic widget, but the augmented widget is efficient. Renegotiation will occur but now there are additional reference points. "Trade the basic widget" is one (as above), but the contract gives an additional reference point of "trade the augmented widget at extra charge p in event E". S can now feel entitled to a similar payoff from the add-on as in event E. Since the gains from trade are higher than in E, S adjusts the reference price upwards to obtain a fraction $\frac{1}{2}(1 + \beta)$ of the increase in the gains. Thus, the additional reference price p_S'' for S in state s_i is determined by

$$p_S'' - c_i = p - c_j + \frac{1}{2}(1 + \beta)(G_i - G_j), \tag{10}$$

where j denotes a reference state in E. Since E contains several states, S can justify using any of them as a reference point. We will take the position that each party is self-serving in his or her choice of reference point, that is, S will use the reference point that gives an argument for the highest price, while B will do the opposite. It is easy to check that (2) and $\beta \in [0, 1)$ imply that the right-hand side of (10) is decreasing in j. Thus, S will base the additional reference price on s_1 and accordingly

$$p_S'' = p + c_i - c_1 + \frac{1}{2}(1 + \beta)(G_i - G_1). \tag{11}$$

Similarly, in choosing whether to use "trade the basic widget" or "trade the augmented widget at extra charge p in event E" as the reference point S adopts the most favorable interpretation for her, that is, she feels entitled to a price equal to

$$Max(p_S', p_S''). \tag{12}$$

Finally, following Hart and Moore (2008) we suppose that S recognizes that B will never pay more than v_i for the add-on in s_i. Hence, S's entitlement is capped by v_i and we can write S's entitlement as

$$Min[v_i, Max(p_S', p_S'')] \tag{13}$$

By a similar logic B thinks that S is entitled to a fraction $\frac{1}{2}(1 - \beta)$ of the increase in the gains from renegotiation and so feels entitled to pay

$$Min\left(p'_B, p''_B\right), \tag{14}$$

where

$$p''_B = p + c_i - c_j + \frac{1}{2}(1 - \beta)(G_i - G_j), \tag{15}$$

and j is a reference state in E. Given that the right-hand side of (15) is decreasing in j, B bases the additional reference point on s_r since it gives an argument for the lowest price and therefore

$$p''_B = p + c_i - c_r + \frac{1}{2}(1 - \beta)(G_i - G_r). \tag{16}$$

Thus, the parties have the opposite preferences regarding the additional reference points. B would use trade in s_r as the reference point because it gives a low price, while S would adopt a reference price based on s_1.

Furthermore, B's entitlement is bounded below by c_i – he realizes that S will never supply the add-on for less than this. Hence, we can write B's entitlement as

$$Max[c_i, Min\left(p'_B, p''_B\right)]. \tag{17}$$

We may conclude that the expected deadweight losses from contract C, incurred in states $s_{r+1}, \ldots, s_n$, are

$$L_C = \sum_{i=r+1}^{n} \pi_i \theta\{Min[v_i, Max(p'_S, p''_S)] - Max[c_i, Min(p'_B, p''_B)]\}. \tag{18}$$

Lemma 1

The deadweight losses in states $s_{r+1}, \ldots, s_n$ under contract C are at least as great as under contract I. That is, $Min[v_i, Max(p'_S, p''_S)] - Max[c_i, Min(p'_B, p''_B)]$ $\geq p'_S - p'_B$.[13]

Lemma 1 is proved in the Appendix. Under contract I the total aggrievement is equal to the difference in the reference prices, $p'_S - p'_B$. According to Lemma 1, including the verifiable event E in the contract may increase aggrievement in states $s_{r+1}, \ldots, s_n$. This is the case if at least one of the parties uses the additional reference point based on E. For example, if S adopts the additional reference point, it must be because it gives an argument for a higher price, $p''_S > p'_S$, and thus the difference in the parties' reference prices increases

---

[13] Note that if $\beta = 1$, as in Hart and Moore (2008), $p'_S = v_i$ and $p'_B = c_i$ and the additional reference point has no effect on this maximal disagreement.

leading to strictly higher deadweight losses under contract C. This is the case even when $p_S'' > v_i$, that is, $Min[v_i, p_S''] = v_i$, since by (6) $v_i > p_S'$ given $\beta < 1$. On the other hand, if $p_S'' \leq p_S'$, S's entitlement is equal to p_S' both under contract C and contract I.

Whether the additional reference points are used depends importantly on the price contracted for the add-on in event E. Since p_S' and p_B' are independent of p, a sufficiently low p will make p_S'' redundant, $p_S'' < p_S'$, while a sufficiently high p results in $p_B'' > p_B'$. To minimize the deadweight losses, it may be possible to make the additional reference points redundant by choosing p appropriately. Suppose $p_B'' < p_B'$ and $p_S'' < p_S'$ for some p so that B feels entitled to p_B'' and S feels entitled to p_S'. Increasing p by $p_B' - p_B''$ makes the additional reference point redundant for B, while S does not switch to using the additional reference point as long as $p_B' - p_B'' \leq p_S' - p_S''$. (Note that by (11) and (16) p increases p_B'' and p_S'' by equal amounts.) In other words, we can set p so that neither party uses the additional reference point if the difference in the additional reference prices does not exceed the difference in the reference prices based on no trade of the add-on, $p_S'' - p_B'' \leq p_S' - p_B'$. However, if $p_S'' - p_B'' > p_S' - p_B'$, it is impossible to find p such that $p_S'' \leq p_S'$ and $p_B'' \geq p_B'$ and so at least one party will use the additional reference point, increasing aggrievement under contract C.

A numerical example may be helpful. Suppose there are four states $s_0, \ldots, s_3$. E comprises two states, s_1 and s_2. The value and the cost of the add-on is $(10, 6)$ in s_1 and $(c_2 + 4, c_2)$ in s_2, where $c_2 > 6$ as per (2), while in s_3 we have $(50, 40)$. It follows from (6) and (7) that $p_S' = 45 + 5\beta$ and $p_B' = 45 - 5\beta$, while from (11) and (16) $p_S'' = p + 37 + 3\beta$ and $p_B'' = p + 43 - c_2 - 3\beta$. Then the additional reference point is redundant for S, $p_S' > p_S''$, if $p < 8 + 2\beta$, while it is redundant for B, $p_B' < p_B''$, if $p > 2 + c_2 - 2\beta$. Accordingly, it is impossible to find p such that neither party uses the additional reference point if $8 + 2\beta < 2 + c_2 - 2\beta$, or equivalently if $6 - c_2 + 4\beta < 0$. This condition holds if the parties have similar views about surplus division, $\beta = 0$. Furthermore, the condition holds for any β if $c_2 > 10$, that is, s_1 and s_2 are disconnected. Finally, the condition is not satisfied if s_1 and s_2 are almost identical, $c_2 \simeq 6$. In what follows, we show that these results generalize.

Let L_C^{min} be the deadweight loss under contract C when p is chosen optimally. That is,

$$L_C^{min} = Min_p \left\{ \sum_{i=r+1}^{n} \pi_i \theta \left[Min[v_i, Max(p_S', p_S'')] - Max[c_i, Min(p_B', p_B'')] \right] \right\}.$$

$$(19)$$

Then $L_C^{min} > \sum_{i=r+1}^{n} \pi_i \theta \beta G_i$, the deadweight loss in states $s_{r+1}, \dots, s_n$ under contact I, if and only if $p_S'' - p_B'' > p_S' - p_B'$. Applying (6), (7), (11) and (16) we have Lemma 2.

Lemma 2

$L_C^{min} > \sum_{i=r+1}^{n} \pi_i \theta \beta G_i$ if and only if $c_1 - c_r + \frac{1}{2}(1+\beta)G_1 - \frac{1}{2}(1-\beta)G_r < 0$.

It is easy to see that the condition in Lemma 2 holds if β is small enough (e.g., $\beta = 0$). To understand this, note that the verifiable contingency E covers several states and B and S base their entitlements on the opposite extremes. Therefore even if β is zero, the entitlements remain divergent, $p_S'' > p_B''$, while under contract I – which gives just one reference point – B and S agree about the reasonable price, $p_S' = p_B'$.

Lemma 3, which is proved in the Appendix, provides more information.

Lemma 3

(i) $L_C^{min} > \sum_{i=r+1}^{n} \pi_i \theta \beta G_i$ if s_1 and s_r are disconnected.

(ii) Fix v_1, c_1 and v_i, c_i, $i = r+1, \dots, n$. Let (v_i^k) and (c_i^k), $i = 2, \dots, r$, be sequences such that $v_i^k \to v_1$ and $c_i^k \to c_1$ for all $i = 2, \dots, r$ as $k \to \infty$. Then $L_C^{min} \to \sum_{i=r+1}^{n} \pi_i \theta \beta G_i$ as $k \to \infty$.

Lemma 3 shows that the condition in Lemma 2 depends on the ambiguity of event E. According to part (i), if E is so ambiguous that its extreme states are disconnected, including it in the contract increases the deadweight losses in $s_{r+1}, \dots, s_n$. On the other hand, according to part (ii), if E is very precise so that the states it comprises are almost identical, adding it in the contract has a negligible effect on deadweight losses in $s_{r+1}, \dots, s_n$.

One further observation can be made. If β is close to 1, $\sum_{i=r+1}^{n} \pi_i \theta \beta G_i$ is approximately equal to $\sum_{i=r+1}^{n} \pi_i \theta G_i$. Although $L_C^{min} > \sum_{i=r+1}^{n} \pi_i \theta \beta G_i$ when s_1 and s_r are disconnected, also L_C^{min} is approximately equal to $\sum_{i=r+1}^{n} \pi_i \theta G_i = \sum_{i=r+1}^{n} \pi_i \theta (v_i - c_i)$. ($L_C^{min}$ cannot exceed this since S's entitlement is capped by v_i and B's by c_i.) Hence although contract C may be slightly less efficient in the nonverifiable states $s_{r+1}, \dots, s_n$, it will be more efficient in states $s_1, \dots, s_r$ of the verifiable event since it avoids deadweight losses there. Hence, if β is close to 1 C dominates I.

Proposition 1 follows immediately from Lemmas 2 and 3 and the last observation.

Proposition 1

(i) If β is sufficiently small, contract I is strictly superior to contract C.

(ii) Fix π_0. Let (π_i^k) be a sequence of probabilities, $i = 1, \ldots, n$, such that $\sum_{i=1}^{r} \pi_i^k \to 0$ and $\sum_{i=r+1}^{n} \pi_i^k \to 1 - \pi_0$ as $k \to \infty$. Then if states s_1 and s_r are disconnected, contract I is strictly superior to contract C for k sufficiently large.

(iii) Fix v_1, c_1 and v_i, c_i, $i = r+1, \ldots, n$. Let (v_i^k) and (c_i^k), $i = 2, \ldots, r$, be sequences such that $v_i^k \to v_1$ and $c_i^k \to c_1$ for all $i = 2, \ldots, r$ as $k \to \infty$. Then, contract C is strictly superior to contract I for k sufficiently large.

(iv) If β is sufficiently close to 1, contract C is strictly superior to contract I.

Proof

(i) Consider the case $\beta = 0$. Obviously the deadweight losses from contract I are zero. Consider contract C. By Lemma 2 the deadweight losses from contract C are strictly positive, $L_C^{min} > 0$. Therefore Proposition 1(*i*) is true for $\beta = 0$. By continuity it must also be true for β close to 0.

(ii) As $k \to \infty$, the deadweight losses under contract I converge to $L_I = \sum_{i=r+1}^{n} \pi_i \theta \beta G_i$. By Lemma 3(*i*) the deadweight losses under contract C are strictly above L_I, given s_1 and s_r are disconnected. Furthermore, there is no significant benefit from avoiding deadweight losses in E since E occurs with negligible probability. Hence contract I is strictly superior to C in the limit, and, by continuity, for large enough k.

(iii) The proof follows directly from Lemma 3(*ii*), which establishes that $L_C^{min} \to \sum_{i=r+1}^{n} \pi_i \theta \beta G_i$. Contract C is then superior because it avoids deadweight losses in E.

Part (*iv*) was established in the text.

Q.E.D.

Proposition 1 can be understood as follows. If B and S have similar views about what is a reasonable division of surplus then it is efficient to contract only on the basic widget and leave the add-on for later (part (*i*)). The reason is that renegotiation will proceed smoothly if the add-on is required. In contrast if the parties contract on the add-on in certain states then renegotiation in other states becomes problematic because the presence of additional reference points hinders it.

At the other extreme if B and S have very different views about what is reasonable then additional reference points do not hinder renegotiation – it is already as bad as it gets – and so contracting on whatever is possible is desirable (part *(iv)*).

Part *(ii)* says that contracting on unlikely events is undesirable if it makes renegotiation in other states problematic. The benefit of eliminating aggrievement in the unlikely states is small whereas the hindering effect of the additional reference points on renegotiation in other states is large. According to Lemma 3 the hindering effect occurs if event E is so ambiguous that its extreme states are disconnected.

Part *(iii)* shows why it is important for our results that there is some ambiguity about the verifiable contingency. According to Lemma 3 if the states in E are almost identical, including it in the contract does not hinder renegotiation in $s_{r+1}, \ldots, s_n$. Since contract C yields zero deadweight losses in event E, contract C then dominates contract I. It is worth noting that in this case setting p to divide the gains from trade evenly in E achieves $L_C^{min} = \sum_{i=r+1}^{n} \pi_i \theta \beta G_i$. Indeed this result is general. If every verifiable contingency where the add-on is efficient is a single state the price for the add-on in that contingency can be chosen to divide the surplus evenly in that state; and then in an unverifiable contingency none of the reference points will hinder renegotiation given that $\frac{1}{2}(1 + \beta) \geq \frac{1}{2} \geq \frac{1}{2}(1 - \beta)$.

Finally, we have assumed that when there are multiple reference points each party will choose the one most favorable to him or her. One might argue that parties who have similar views about how the surplus is divided – parties for whom β is small – will also agree about what is an appropriate reference point. We can relax our assumption by assuming that each party chooses the most favorable reference point with probability β, while they agree about appropriate reference point with probability $(1 - \beta)$. Therefore, there is no aggrievement with probability $(1 - \beta)$ and the deadweight losses under both contract I and contract C are multiplied by β. Obviously β cancels out in any comparison and does not affect Proposition 1 as long as there is not perfect agreement about appropriate reference points.[14]

4 Large Gains in Event E

We have considered a verifiable event E that groups the states with relatively low gains from trading the add-on. We now analyze the opposite case where the gains are large in E. Specifically, we continue to assume (3) but now suppose that E

---

[14] Alternatively, it can be argued that the two dimensions – division of the surplus and choice of reference point – are distinct. Suppose that a contract says that S will supply B with a widget except if state s occurs. In actuality state s', similar to but different from s, occurs. S might argue that since s' is similar to s she should be excused from supplying. B might argue that precisely because s was mentioned but s' wasn't S should *not* be excused. Such a disagreement seems to have little to do with differences in β.

comprises states $s_{r+1}, \ldots, s_n$, where $r \geq 1$. The difference this makes is that when a party adopts the additional reference point, they need to adjust the reference price *downwards* to reflect the lower gains. Self-serving bias then implies that the parties feel entitled to pass *more* of the reduction in gains to the other party. Thus, S adjusts the reference price downwards only by a fraction $\frac{1}{2}(1-\beta)$ of the losses while B reduces the reference price more than S, by a fraction $\frac{1}{2}(1+\beta)$ of the losses. Accordingly, the additional reference prices are given by[15]

$$p_S'' = c_i + p - c_{r+1} - \frac{1}{2}(1-\beta)(G_{r+1} - G_i), \tag{19}$$

$$p_B'' = c_i + p - c_n - \frac{1}{2}(1+\beta)(G_n - G_i). \tag{20}$$

Now $p_S'' - p_B''$ differs from what it was in Section 3, and the condition in Lemma 2 becomes

$$c_{r+1} - c_n + \frac{1}{2}(1-\beta)G_{r+1} - \frac{1}{2}(1+\beta)G_n + 2\beta G_i < 0. \tag{21}$$

Note that (21) depends on the current state s_i unlike the condition in Lemma 2. This will not change some of our results, for example (21) is satisfied for $\beta = 0$. However, it does change part (*iii*) of Proposition 1 since there can be deadweight losses in s_i even if there is no ambiguity about E.

To understand this, suppose that E consists of only one state, s_n. Then (21) simplifies to

$$G_i - \frac{1}{2}G_n < 0. \tag{22}$$

(22) does not depend on β. Then including E in the contract hinders renegotiation in s_i for all values of β despite the fact that there is no ambiguity in E. Note that in this case $p_S'' - p_B'' = \beta(G_n - G_i)$, while $p_S' - p_B' = \beta G_i$ as previously. Small G_i then implies that there is a lot to argue about under contract C, while there is little to argue about under contract I, which is why even a precise E causes problems.[16] However, if the gains in the unverifiable states are not very small, $G_i \geq \frac{1}{2}G_n$ for all $i = 1, \ldots, r$, then including a precise E in the contract is beneficial. Under this additional condition contract C dominates I as in Proposition 1 *(iii)*.

---

[15] Equations (19) and (20) also take into account that the parties base their reference prices on the opposite extreme states of E.

[16] In Section 3 where the gains are low in E a similar effect does not arise because large G_i implies that there is a lot to argue under both contract C and contract I.

Proposition 2

Assume that E comprises states $s_{r+1}, \ldots, s_n$, where $r \geq 1$, and that (3) holds.

(i) If β is sufficiently small, contract I is strictly superior to contract C.

(ii) Fix π_0. Let (π_i^k) be a sequence of probabilities, $i = 1, \ldots, n$, such that $\sum_{i=1}^r \pi_i^k \to 1 - \pi_0$ and $\sum_{i=r+1}^n \pi_i^k \to 0$ as $k \to \infty$. Then if states s_{r+1} and s_n are disconnected, contract I is strictly superior to contract C for k sufficiently large.

(iii) Fix v_n, c_n and v_i, c_i, $i = 1, \ldots, r$. Let (v_i^k) and (c_i^k), $i = r+1, \ldots, n$, be sequences such that $v_i^k \to v_n$ and $c_i^k \to c_n$ for all $i = r+1, \ldots, n-1$ as $k \to \infty$. Then, if $G_i \geq \frac{1}{2} G_n$ for all $i = 1, \ldots, r$, contract C is strictly superior to contract I for k sufficiently large.

(iv) If β is sufficiently close to 1, contract C is strictly superior to contract I.

It is helpful to illustrate the role of the assumption $G_i \geq \frac{1}{2} G_n$ using a numerical example. Suppose that E comprises a state s_n where the value and the cost of the add-on are $(50, 40)$, while in the current state s_i they are $(10, 6)$, violating the condition $G_i \geq \frac{1}{2} G_n$. Then according to (6) and (7) $p_S' = 8 + 2\beta$ and $p_B' = 8 - 2\beta$, while from (19) and (20) $p_S'' = p - 37 + 3\beta$ and $p_B'' = p - 37 - 3\beta$. Then $p_S' \geq p_S''$ if $p \leq 45 - \beta$, while $p_B' \leq p_B''$ if $p \geq 45 + \beta$. Thus, there is no such p that the additional reference point is redundant for both parties even though there is no ambiguity about E. In contrast, if we replace $(50, 40)$ by $(46, 40)$, which satisfies $G_i \geq \frac{1}{2} G_n$, then it is easy to check that $43 - \beta \leq p \leq 43 + \beta$ ensures that the additional reference points are redundant.

It is also instructive to use this example to reconsider the case in Section 3, where the gains from trade are low in E. Reverse the numbers so that $(10, 6)$ in E and $(50, 40)$ in the current state. Suppose also that the parties contract for $p = 8$ for trading the add-on in E, so that each party's payoff equals 2 in event E. Then $p_S' = 45 + 5\beta$ and $p_B' = 45 - 5\beta$, while from (11) and (16) $p_S'' = 45 + 3\beta$ and $p_B'' = 45 - 3\beta$. Clearly neither party adopts the additional reference point. The example confirms the observation made in Section 3 that, when the gains from trade are low in E and E contains only one state, dividing the surplus evenly in that state avoids problems in other states.

5 Summary and Conclusions

In this Element, we have investigated when and why parties will deliberately write incomplete contracts even when contract-writing costs are zero. We have argued that adding a contingency of the form, "The buyer will require an extra good or service in event E," has a benefit and a cost. The benefit is that there is less to argue about in event E; the cost is that the reference point provided by the extra service in event E may increase argument costs in states outside E.

Our principal result is that the relative benefit and cost of adding a contingency will be sensitive to how closely the parties agree about what is a reasonable division of surplus when an incomplete contract is renegotiated. The benefit can exceed the cost when parties have very different views about what is a reasonable division of surplus, but the opposite will be the case if they have shared views. Under the latter conditions an incomplete contract will be strictly optimal.

It is worth considering how our theory's implications differ from those of a theory based on asymmetric information. Consider the wage indexation example in the introduction. If an employee is offered a contract whereby the wage is indexed on some signal, the employee might think that the employer already knows that the signal will be such that the employee's wage is low, making the contract less attractive. But this would suggest that in an optimal contract the wage should not vary much with the index, not that it should not vary at all. Only by introducing costs of contractual clauses (as in Spier [1992]) can one explain a complete lack of indexation.[17]

In contrast in our theory, introducing a contingency has a discontinuous effect: it introduces a brand new reference point. We have seen that in some circumstances the cost of doing this outweighs the benefit.

Our theory also has different implications from the asymmetric information one regarding the timing of incompleteness. Signaling favorable private information is particularly important at the beginning of a relationship. In our theory one possible explanation for similar views about the division of surplus is the history of the relationship between the buyer and the seller. If the parties have interacted before they may have grown to know and like each other, with the implication that each will become more generous about sharing surplus (see the social influence theory of Kelman [1958]). Therefore we would expect contracts to become less complete in long-term relationships, but be more complete when such relationships are formed – in contrast to the asymmetric information theory.[18]

---

[17] In Hartman-Glaser and Hebert (2020) asymmetric information is about the quality of the index rather than the fundamentals. Under that assumption non-indexation can result in a competitive equilibrium – without any writing costs – as a single principal cannot convince the agent that the index is of high quality if all the other principals offer a non-indexed contract. However, non-indexation is not an equilibrium in their setup if asymmetric information is about the fundamentals and the index is known to be of good quality.

[18] However, a complete analysis would have to incorporate the possibility that parties will anticipate this potential warming at the beginning of their relationship, which would complicate matters considerably.

Finally, our approach may also be able to explain why parties often use general rather than specific language in contracts. For example, parties negotiating acquisitions frequently include a clause that excuses the buyer if the target seller suffers a "material adverse change" (see Schwartz and Scott [2010]). According to our theory the advantage of a general clause is that it creates a neutral reference point: it is like describing states $s_1, \ldots, s_n$, rather than event E, as a situation where the add-on should be provided. In contrast spelling out particular contingencies that qualify as a material adverse change may complicate renegotiation in other contingencies that are not easily described but where the parties also intended to excuse the buyer. Asymmetric information theories do not seem to have much to say about this issue.

Our results depend on how similar or different views the parties have about the division of surplus. It is natural to ask what determines empirically whether parties' views about the division of surplus are likely to be similar or different. At this point we do not have a very good answer to this question. It seems reasonable that it has something to do with norms, trust, social capital, and empathy. A "dog-eat-dog" world may be one where each party feels entitled to the best outcome possible. A more civilized world may be one where sharing the surplus from renegotiation comes more naturally. The vast empirical and experimental literature on ultimatum, dictator, and public goods games (see, e.g., Camerer [2003]) suggests that views of a reasonable division of surplus may vary across countries, societies, and so on, in a systematic way. Our theory predicts that one should expect to see less complete contracts in situations where people are more empathetic toward each other and more complete contracts when people are less empathetic.

Some guidance about the importance of shared views for building trust can be obtained from the relationship marketing literature (Morgan and Hunt [1994]). Trust has two dimensions: credibility and benevolence. The first is related to ideas formalized in the repeated games literature in economics (see Malcomson [2013] for a survey). The second is concerned with shared values as trust develops through interpreting and assessing whether the other party is interested in his partner's best interests. Parties with shared values have a similar definition of what behaviors and policies are appropriate and can therefore better understand what drives the partner's behavior (see the attribution theory of Heider [1958]).

More recently, Frydlinger et al. (2019) and Frydlinger and Hart (2024) examine theoretically and in case studies formal relational contracts which spell out the guiding principles – such as equity, loyalty and honesty – to be applied in any renegotiations. Central to these contracts are lengthy *ex-ante* discussions regarding the guiding principles in order to form shared views.

As mentioned in the introduction, there is a sizeable law and economics literature on contractual incompleteness. We have noted that one difference between our Element and this literature is that the literature tends to assume a fixed cost of writing or enforcing contractual clauses. To understand other differences it is useful to make the distinction introduced in Ayres and Gertner (1992) between "obligationally incomplete" and "insufficiently state contingent" contracts. The first refer to contracts that cannot be enforced as they stand or are ambiguous, for example, a contract might require S to supply a widget to B even in a situation where this is impossible; or might require S to supply a widget by a particular time but not say what should happen if S fails to do this. Some sort of judicial (or outside) interpretation seems required to complete such a contract (if the parties fail to agree about what should happen). The second – insufficiently state contingent – refers to a contract that is fully specified in all circumstances but which does not contain all the contingent clauses that the parties would like. In this case the parties do not require judicial (or outside) intervention (although they might benefit from it).

Our Element is about the second situation rather than the first, whereas much of the law and economics literature is about the first (see, e.g., Shavell [1980], Ayres and Gertner [1989, 1992]). Indeed we have ignored the role of courts (or other outsiders, such as arbitrators) in interpreting contracts. In future work it would be desirable to introduce the courts. A well-functioning judicial system may allow the parties to economize on the number of contingencies they include themselves, thereby reducing the number of reference points. The parties can rely on the courts to tell them what to do in some verifiable states; while in other states renegotiation may proceed smoothly given that the judicial solution may loom less large as a reference point than a party-induced remedy.

An analysis of legal rules in a world where parties write incomplete contracts for the kinds of reasons explored here is an interesting and challenging topic for future research.

Appendix

Proof of Lemma 1

Suppose first that $p_S'' > p_S'$ so that S uses the additional reference point under contract C. S's entitlement is then $Min(v_i, p_S'')$ which is strictly greater than p_S' since by (6) $v_i > p_S'$ given $\beta < 1$. While if $p_S'' \leq p_S'$, S's entitlement is given by $Min(v_i, p_S')$ and is equal to p_S' both under contract C and contract I.

In a similar manner B uses the additional reference point under contract C if $p_B'' < p_B'$ resulting in entitlement of $Max(c_i, p_B'') < p_B'$ since by (7) $p_B' > c_i$ given $\beta < 1$. While if $p_B'' \geq p_B'$, B does not use the additional reference point and his entitlement equals p_B' under both contracts.

Q.E.D.

Proof of Lemma 3

(i) According to Lemma 2, $L_C^{min} > \sum_{i=r+1}^{n} \pi_i \theta \beta G_i$ if and only if

$$c_1 - c_r + \frac{1}{2}(1 + \beta)G_1 - \frac{1}{2}(1 - \beta)G_r < 0. \tag{A.1}$$

It is straightforward to show that (A.1) holds if $\beta = 0$. For $\beta \to 1$ (A.1) approaches

$$c_1 - c_r + G_1 = v_1 - c_r < 0. \tag{A.2}$$

(A.2) is satisfied if s_1 and s_r are disconnected. In this case (A.1) is satisfied for all β since it is linear in β.

(ii) As $k \to \infty$ the left-hand side of (A.1) approaches

$$\frac{1}{2}\beta G_1 + \frac{1}{2}\beta G_r > 0. \tag{A.3}$$

Hence (A.1) is eventually violated for any $\beta > 0$. Furthermore, if $\beta = 0$, it is easy to see that $p_S'' - p_B'' \to 0$ and so $L_C^{min} \to 0$. Accordingly, $L_C^{min} \to \sum_{i=r+1}^{n} \pi_i \theta \beta G_i$ as $k \to \infty$.

Q.E.D.

Proof of Proposition 2

(i) In Section 4, we established that $L_C^{min} > \sum_{i=1}^{r} \pi_i \theta \beta G_i$ if and only if

$$c_{r+1} - c_n + \frac{1}{2}(1 - \beta)G_{r+1} - \frac{1}{2}(1 + \beta)G_n + 2\beta G_i < 0. \tag{A.4}$$

It is straightforward to show that (A.4) is satisfied if $\beta = 0$. Thus the proof of Proposition 1(i) applies.

(ii) If $\beta \to 1$, (A.4) approaches

$$c_{r+1} - c_n - G_n + 2G_i < 0, \tag{A.5}$$

which is equivalent to

$$G_i < \frac{1}{2}(v_n - c_{r+1}). \tag{A.6}$$

Therefore, if (A.6) is satisfied, (A.4) holds for all β.

Note that, if $G_i \geq \frac{1}{2}(v_n - c_{r+1})$, then

$$v_n - c_n + v_{r+1} - c_{r+1} = G_n + G_{r+1} > 2G_i \geq v_n - c_{r+1}, \tag{A.7}$$

and so $v_{r+1} > c_n$, that is, the extreme states of E are overlapping. Thus, if the extreme states of E are disconnected, (A.6) is satisfied. Accordingly, (A.4) holds for all β if s_n and s_{r+1} are disconnected. Therefore, we can apply the proof of Proposition 1(ii).

(iii) As $k \to \infty$ (A.4) approaches

$$-\beta G_n + 2\beta G_i < 0. \tag{A.8}$$

Therefore, $L_C^{min} \to \sum_{i=1}^{r} \pi_i \theta \beta G_i$ if $G_i \geq \frac{1}{2}G_n$ as long as $\beta > 0$. Furthermore, if $\beta = 0$, it is easy to see that $p_S'' - p_B'' \to 0$ and so $L_C^{min} \to 0$.

(iv) Proposition 2(iv) can be established by a similar argument to Proposition 1 (iv).

Q.E.D.

References

Aghion, Philippe and Patrick Bolton. 1987. "Contracts as a Barrier to Entry." *American Economic Review* 77(3): 388–401.

Aghion, Philippe and Benjamin Hermalin. 1990. "Legal Restrictions on Private Contracts Can Enhance Efficiency." *Journal of Law, Economics and Organizations* 6(2): 381–409.

Al-Najjar, Nabil I., Luca Anderlini and Leonardo Felli. 2006. "Undescribable Events." *Review of Economic Studies* 73(4): 849–868.

Anderlini, Luca and Leonardo Felli. 1994. "Incomplete Written Contracts: Undescribable States of Nature." *Quarterly Journal of Economics* 109(4): 1085–1124.

Ayres, Ian and Robert Gertner. 1989. "Filling Gaps in Incomplete Contracts: An Economic Theory of Default Rules." *Yale Law Journal* 99(1): 87–130.

Ayres, Ian and Robert Gertner. 1992. "Strategic Contractual Inefficiency and the Optimal Choice of Legal Rules." *Yale Law Journal* 101(4): 729–773.

Bajari, Patrick and Steven Tadelis. 2001. "Incentives versus Transaction Costs: A Theory of Procurement Contracts." *Rand Journal of Economics* 32(3): 387–407.

Baker, George, Robert Gibbons and Kevin J. Murphy. 1994. "Subjective Performance Measures in Optimal Incentive Contracts." *Quarterly Journal of Economics* 109(4): 1125–1156.

Benabou, Roland and Jean Tirole. 2003. "Intrinsic and Extrinsic Motivation." *Review of Economic Studies* 70(3): 489–520.

Benabou, Roland and Jean Tirole. 2006. "Incentives and Prosocial Behavior." *American Economic Review* 96(5): 1652–1678.

Bernheim, B. Douglas and Michael D. Whinston. 1998. "Incomplete Contracts and Strategic Ambiguity." *American Economic Review* 88(4): 902–932.

Bolton, Patrick and Antoine Faure-Grimaud. 2010. "Satisficing Contracts." *Review of Economic Studies* 77(3): 937–971.

Camerer, Colin. 2003. *Behavioral Game Theory*. Princeton: Princeton University Press.

Card, David. 1986. "An Empirical Model of Wage Indexation Provisions in Union Contracts." *Journal of Political Economy* 94(3): S144–S175.

Chakravarty, Surajeet and W. Bentley MacLeod. 2009. "Contracting in the Shadow of the Law." *Rand Journal of Economics* 40(3): 533–557.

Che, Yeon-Koo and Donald Hausch. 1999. "Cooperative Investments and the Value of Contracting." *American Economic Review* 89(1): 125–147.

Dye, Ronald. 1985. "Costly Contract Contingencies." *International Economic Review* 26(1): 233–250.

Fehr, Ernst, Oliver Hart and Christian Zehnder. 2015. "How Do Informal Agreements and Renegotiation Shape Contractual Reference Points?" *Journal of the European Economic Association* 13(1): 1–15.

Frydlinger, David, Oliver Hart and Kate Vitasek. 2019. "A New Approach to Contracts." *Harvard Business Review* September–October.

Frydlinger, David and Oliver Hart. 2024. "Overcoming Contractual Incompleteness: The Role of Guiding Principles." *Journal of Law, Economics, and Organization* forthcoming.

Halonen-Akatwijuka, Maija and Oliver Hart. 2020. "Continuing Contracts." *Journal of Law, Economics, and Organization* 36(2): 284–313.

Hart, Oliver and John Moore. 1999. "Foundations of Incomplete Contracts." *Review of Economic Studies* 66(1): 115–38

Hart, Oliver and John Moore. 2008. "Contracts as Reference Points." *Quarterly Journal of Economics* 123(1): 1–48.

Hartman-Glaser, Barney and Benjamin Hébert. 2020. "The Insurance Is the Lemon: Failing to Index Contracts." *Journal of Finance* 75(1): 463–506.

Heider, Fritz. 1958. *The Psychology of Interpersonal Relations*. Hillside (NJ): Erlbaum.

Herold, Florian. 2010. "Contractual Incompleteness as a Signal of Trust." *Games and Economic Behavior* 68: 180–191.

Herweg, Fabian and Klaus M. Schmidt. 2015. "Loss Aversion and Ex Post Inefficient Renegotiation." *Review of Economic Studies* 82(1): 297–332.

Kelman, Herbert C. 1958. "Compliance, Identification, and Internalization: Three Processes of Attitude Change." *The Journal of Conflict Resolution* 2(1): 51–60.

Kvaløy, Ola and Trond E. Olsen. 2009. "Endogenous Verifiability and Relational Contracting." *American Economic Review* 99: 2193–2208.

Malcomson, James. 2013. "Relational Incentive Contracts." In *The Handbook of Organizational Economics*, edited by Robert Gibbons and John Roberts, 1014–1065. Princeton: Princeton University Press.

Morgan, Robert M. and Shelby D. Hunt. 1994. "The Commitment-Trust Theory of Relationship Marketing." *Journal of Marketing* 58(3): 20–38.

Oyer, Paul. 2004. "Why Do Firms Use Incentives that Have No Incentive Effects?" *Journal of Finance* 59(4): 1619–1649.

Posner, Richard. 1986. *The Economic Analysis of Law*. Boston: Little, Brown.

Rothschild, Michael and Joseph Stiglitz. 1976. "Equilibrium in Competitive Insurance Markets: An Essay on the Economics of Imperfect Information." *Quarterly Journal of Economics* 90(4): 629–649.

Schmidt, Klaus M. and Monika Schnitzer. 1995. "The Interaction of Explicit and Implicit Contracts." *Economics Letters* 48(2): 193–199.

Schwartz, Alan and Robert E. Scott. 2010. "Contract Interpretation Redux." *Yale Law Journal* 119: 926–964.

Segal, Ilya. 1999. "Complexity and Renegotiation: A Foundation for Incomplete Contracts." *Review of Economic Studies* 66(1): 57–82.

Shavell, Steven. 1980. "Damage Measures for Breach of Contract." *Bell Journal of Economics* 11(2): 466–490.

Spier, Kathryn. 1992. "Incomplete Contracts and Signalling." *RAND Journal of Economics* 23(3): 432–443.

Tirole, Jean. 2009. "Cognition and Incomplete Contracts." *American Economic Review* 99(1):265–294.

Weitzman, Martín L. 1984. *The Share Economy: Conquering Stagflation.* Cambridge, MA: Harvard University Press.

Williamson, Oliver E. 1985. *The Economic Institutions of Capitalism.* New York: Macmillan.

Acknowledgments

We would like to thank Philippe Aghion, Ola Kvaløy, Evagelos Pafilis, Klaus Schmidt, and particularly Kathy Spier for very helpful comments. We also thank the editor and three referees for valuable comments. The first author gratefully acknowledges financial support from the Norwegian Research Council.

Cambridge Elements ⹀

Law, Economics and Politics

Elements in the Series

A full series listing is available at: www.cambridge.org/ELEP

Printed in the United States
by Baker & Taylor Publisher Services